FROM THE NOTEBOOK
of a NEW YORKER
Simplicity in a Complex World

> No need to be PESSIMISTIC... It wouldn't work anyway :)

DAVID A. ROTMAN

From the Notebook of a New Yorker
Simplicity in a Complex World
by David A. Rotman

Copyright © 2025 by David A. Rotman

Published by David A. Rotman Books
davidarotmanbooks@gmail.com

No part of this publication may be reproduced, stored in a retrieval system, or transmitted in any form or by any means—electronic, mechanical, photocopying, recording, or otherwise—without prior written permission from the author, except in the case of brief quotations used in critical articles or reviews.

This is a work of nonfiction. Any references to the thoughts, experiences, or spiritual insights of the author are based on personal understanding.

For inquiries, contact the author directly at
davidarotmanbooks@gmail.com

Edited: Dr. Anouk Shambrook, Janis Baron, and Kathy Stroud

Book and cover design: Chris Molé Design

Front cover image: David Rotman holding hands with his grandmother Baba (also known as Rose Rind), circa 1951, Bronx, New York. Courtesy of the author

Library of Congress Control Number: 2025914976

ISBN: 979-8-9994489-0-3

Printed in the United States of America

David and his wife Elizabeth (Liz) share joy on their wedding day. Liz was the impetus behind David publishing his book.

I dedicate this small volume to my soul mate and wife, Elizabeth, and children Staci, Michael, Rachel, and Mira, all of whom have provided my most important lessons of Love, which, after all, are the purest expressions of Divinity that we can manifest.

I also dedicate it to those participating in the "meditation group," over seventy people over the last forty years who have participated in meditations and discussions that I generally led, to my best friend and teacher—now deceased—David Pomerantz, and to Jahnavi Barker and Janis Baron, who have supported us all with their Love and organizational skills.

Contents

Foreword vii
Introduction xiii
Chapter 1: How It All Began 1
Chapter 2: The Basic Untruths 3
Chapter 3: The Source of It All 7
Chapter 4: Cleaning Up the Gears 9
Chapter 5: Receptivity 15
Photo Gallery 25
Chapter 6: The Unfolding Vision 37
Chapter 7: Learning the Lessons 41
Chapter 8: The Mechanisms of Release 49
Chapter 9: Our Immediate Needs 55
Chapter 10: Stability 61
Chapter 11: Rules of the Road 65
Chapter 12: It All Comes Back to Now 79
Chapter 13: Love 81
Postscript: Still a Young New Yorker 85
Acknowledgements 87
About the Author 89

This photo of David's Meditation Group at a retreat, sometime around 1990, depicts the joy and sense of camaraderie everyone felt (and still feels) when together. The foreword that follows was written by members of that group.

Foreword

By Dr. Anouk Shambrook and Janis Baron

WHAT HAPPENS WHEN A BRONX-RAISED LAWYER—trained in logic, raised on stickball, and fluent in New York skepticism—turns inward to explore the nature of reality, truth, and love?

That question didn't end with an answer. It began a lifetime of exploration—and this book tells its story.

From the Notebook of a New Yorker is part spiritual memoir, part field guide to being human. In clear, unpretentious prose laced with playful humor, David Rotman invites us into reckoning with life's biggest questions:

- Why are we here?
- What is the purpose of pain?
- How do we live from love instead of fear?

David grew up in the Bronx. His path didn't begin with robes, rituals, or years in a monastery. It began, of all things, with a stranger and a spontaneous act of generosity—followed by a moment of wordless, world-tilting awareness. Not your typical enlightenment origin story. But it got his attention.

That moment sparked a decades-long exploration, one grounded not in dogma, but in practice. And not practiced in seclusion, but woven into the mess, beauty, and heartbreak of everyday life. David writes about lawsuits and grandmothers, India and the streets of the Bronx, openness and humility, discipline and presence. This is not the voice of a distant mystic. It's the voice of someone who has lived deeply, stumbled plenty, and dared to look—really look—at what's here.

This book won't try to fix you. It won't push beliefs or promise five easy steps to bliss. It offers something deeper and, we think, more powerful: A mirror. A nudge. A fierce but gentle invitation to stop chasing and start listening—to your own life, to this moment, to the wisdom that might already be humming quietly inside you.

Traditionally, a foreword is written by an acclaimed expert. We're not here to claim anything—except maybe our seats in the circle. We're two students *of many* who've been transformed by spending decades in the field of awareness David naturally creates—Janis for almost forty years and Anouk for over twenty. We've practiced with him, learning over time to stay present and in our hearts, even as he tested us by trying to distract us with humorous stories or irresistible logic. Again and again, we watched how he pointed us—gently and relentlessly—into the simplicity that's already here. We figured you would want to know what kind of man is behind the chapters you're about to read.

Through meditation groups and workshops,

through tears, laughter, illness, celebration, and change, we've seen it and known it firsthand. We listened to his stories and his teachings, delved into his guided meditations, and then went back into the world, doing our best to apply what we'd understood. And we can say with great love (and a little awe): Our lives have changed. Dramatically. Often in ways we didn't think were possible.

So, yes—this is a foreword. But it's also a heartfelt testament to a man who's changed so many of our lives.

He's not just another voice in the spiritual or self-help world. He's *the real deal.* Not because he says so. He has never said so. It's because of the way his presence ripples into the people around him.

Since he first started leading meditations back in 1984—in the modest living room of his San Francisco apartment—hundreds of people came and went. But over seventy of us stuck around—for decades. He guided us through literally hundreds of grace-filled, inspired meditations, personal processes, and interactive teaching sessions. He also taught through long, often intense retreats held on land in the mountains north of San Francisco.

David has long said that the best way to evaluate a teacher is to look at the students. Are they growing? Are they more loving? Do they get better or worse? In the case of so many of us in David's Meditation Group, the answer is a resounding yes. We've become *more* grounded, *more* honest, *more* able to be with pain and joy. We've let go of things we thought we'd carry forever. We've found longer stretches of peace. Not perfection—but peace.

Many of us have done big work in the world as an outgrowth of the inner alignment that took shape through our time with David—rooted in embodied presence, deepened by loving awareness, and carried by the quiet confidence to be with whatever arises. Every session felt, in some way, life-changing for someone. That inner shift translated into outer change. Many of the group members became healers, teachers, creatives, and leaders across nonprofit and business sectors. Others healed relationships and longstanding trauma, becoming more at peace, happier, and more able to show up in healthy, supportive ways for others.

And it's not just us. David's presence seems to quietly uplift countless people who encounter him—often without them realizing why. He's even been known to resolve corporate battles once thought completely intractable. (We think of it as *Zen and the Art of Mediating Multi-Million-Dollar Disputes.*)

What David carries—what he shares—is not a technique. It's a transmission. He points us, again and again, *not to his truth*, but to *ours*. You see, David carries peace with him. And his peace is so radiant that we *feel* it. It amplifies the latent peace in us and invites us inward—to find whatever else might be waiting there. David has said over and over: "Allow." And in that spirit, we uncover our own riches inside.

We're so grateful to finally share this with you. Our only advice? *Don't just read this book with your mind.* Let this book reach your body, your heart, your *inner knowing.* David has *lived* what he writes and he has made it possible for us—and countless others—to live it. He's not selling you a philosophy. He's inviting you into Presence.

May this book meet you where you are, walk beside you for a while, and remind you—gently, fiercely, and with a wink—that what you're seeking might already be here.

Hilda Charlton was David's beloved teacher. She showed him what it was like to live in the moment and to live from Divinity. She instructed him to start the meditation group.

Introduction

My own journey began long, long ago, I found, in a time I only distantly remember. It is with a deep appreciation and thanks for those who have stayed with me in my wanderings, my uncertainties and my fears that I now take pen to paper.

I titled this book "From the Notebook of a New Yorker," even though there was no actual, physical notebook that recorded these events. The notebook is my reflections on how I remember the turning points in my life.

Although I have not lived in New York for many decades, I grew up there, interacting directly with a wide variety of people, learning to be open to the complexity and diversity of their lives and points of view. I liked New York. I respected it and still feel it inside. The openness and directness there made possible my embrace of some very substantial changes in the way I saw the world as I moved away and into my twenties.

I left New York when college and then law school called. But still, the perspective I had gained through my childhood in New York led to the experiences that have informed this book.

I grew up doing the ordinary things kids did in New York, playing stickball, punchball and roller skate hockey in the streets of the Bronx, and basketball in the school yards. Because I was not programmed with fixed beliefs, my mind stayed open. Finally, one day, years later, one of the startling things my mind opened to was a state of profound joy I had never felt before. I came to that feeling—call it an "awakening" —not from wanting it, conjuring it or planning how to acquire it; I feel that it was simply a gift.

That awakening experience opened me to a feeling I didn't know existed and that I wanted more of. I believe that wanting it and being open to it is what brought my most significant teacher, Hilda, into my life.

Hilda Charlton spent eighteen years of her life living in India, and came back to New York to teach what she had become. Anyone could join her on Thursday evenings at Synod House in the Cathedral of St. John the Divine. Hilda showed me what it was like to live in the moment and to live from Divinity. And I was open to all she taught because the New Yorker in me was not afraid.

I followed Hilda around for eight years, inhaling all of her actions, all of her words. She was a teacher to thousands of people, each one curious to know more truth about themselves and life. But more importantly, she lived the truth she taught and you could see that. Contact with her opened forgotten places in me and changed my life completely. That connection led me to India three times, where I lived in ashrams and met others who lived from inside themselves in a way I had not known existed. The experience was a journey back to myself and my true roots. Everything you read in this book is a result of that opening.

It is commonplace now for us to think of our roots. We think of them as a place, a heritage, a family. My roots are like these, except I have found that they are not limited in the way I thought they might be. Rather than finding my heritage limited to a particular family tree or group of ancestors, I have found that my heritage is life, my family is humanity, and my family tree is rooted in God. All of which is quite a series of discoveries for a kid from New York.

The chapters you are about to enter are intended to carry the reader along on the journey that I began many years ago. It's about the series of openings that I allowed to change me completely.

My life has transformed since those days on the streets of New York, and yet still I feel the New Yorker in me. It is in me to share with you what I have learned—from teachers, from my own inner knowing, from my experience in applying the wisdom to my life, and from my own teaching. This expression of my truth is not something that I conceived in my mind; it's something I feel the Universe has given me—and I am tremendously grateful. I pass it on, as best I can, to you.

~ David A. Rotman, 2025

From the Notebook *of a* New Yorker

CHAPTER ONE

How It All Began

I HAVE ALWAYS FELT, THAT IN SIMPLICITY, we would find Truth, and that absolute Truth is utterly simple. Perhaps the plain truth of our beginning is this: It's the very nature of the **All That Is**—what I call God—to express itself fully. Creation is that expression, and manifestation is its inevitable result.

If we accept the possibility that this simple explanation is true, then it is also possible that we all, as individuals, partake of God and are co-creators with God. Manifestation is a combination of what we bring forth and what God brings forth. I have come to these conclusions in fifty years of not thinking about them, but gradually seeing where these assumptions take me, noticing how this partnership with God affects my life and those lives around me. I have found that starting with this worldview has resulted in a full and rich life for me and for others who adopt it.

This book is about manifesting, about how the world is created and how we play a role in that. It is about how you can more effectively create the life you wish to live.

I ask that you read this book with your heart open. There is a very good chance that you, like many others, may also feel its truth.

CHAPTER TWO

The Basic Untruths

It is the utter simplicity of Truth that makes it so hard to comprehend. We are all accustomed to understanding with our minds, and our minds have been trained to "think." For my money, thinking is a major source of our problems. We insist on reasons and explanations when, in fact, Truth is completely independent of reason; it simply exists. It makes no difference to Truth whether the mind accepts it or not. Truth does not care a whit whether reason confirms its existence. It simply is. Yet the mind seeks explanation, and so, to satisfy the mind, we have evolved a series of "explanations" concerning the nature of ourselves, the universe, energy, life, God and everything else that seems to make a difference to us. Yet, the more we say, the more, of necessity, we must dilute Truth with reason. Every dilution of Truth creates untruth. Every explanation given to satisfy the mind misstates Truth.

What a quandary! How then are we to spread the Truth, if we cannot speak of it without lying? We cannot spread the Truth by speaking of it, only by *Living It*. The only justification for books seeking to spread Truth (including this one) is the hope that by expressing thoughts that have kernels of truth, a few people will change their actions.

I should also note, for those among you who seek to write, that the act of writing a relatively high truth clarifies and makes that truth stronger in the world. When it is read and comprehended, it gains further strength, but only when it is lived and expressed in actions, words and thoughts does it really become part of the fabric of our physical reality. I have found it very interesting that, for the first years the meditation group functioned, we spoke a great deal. Now, almost all our time is spent in meditation; even when we speak, it comes from the same place as our meditations.

It should now be clear that much of what I or anyone else writes on this subject is only a distant cousin to Truth. This language and our minds are, however, all we have to work with in this medium, so understanding these limitations lets us go forward.

David's grandmother, "Baba," was the formative influence in his life. Here she poses with David when he was 6 years old.

CHAPTER THREE

The Source of It All

I BEGAN BY EMPHASIZING THE UNITY OF CREATION, the All That Is. This is obviously the source of it all. But, how are we to work with that source within ourselves and express it to the world? How are we to get in touch with, stay in touch with and be guided by that source within ourselves? These questions are asked over and over again, frequently by the same person. The answer is simply to seek the truth within ourselves and express it. I am afraid that this answer, while it may get an A for accuracy, probably only rates a D for helpfulness. It doesn't provide much assistance to the person who says, "Yes, I understand the goal, but how do I do that, how do I know what is true, how do I find it, and how do I recognize it in myself?"

All are good questions. The basic touchstone of the answer is: "It varies." It varies because what any particular person must learn depends on that person, and the state of his or her evolution and history. Each person learns the same lessons, wins the same victories and suffers the same defeats, but all in their own particular, unique way. No two people on the planet have ever done it the same way, and they never will. While we are all essentially the same at the source, each of our expressions of that source is inherently different. Thus have arisen the sometimes bewildering array of religions, consciousness processes, and schools of spiritual development which seem to be saying the same thing, but in such different words that it is sometimes difficult to be sure. In essence, those that are truly based on Truth must all be saying the same thing because Truth is one, however diverse its expression. How does one decide which of these expressions of Truth will lead him or her home?

This is possible only by developing that internal guidance system within us all that knows Truth and moves toward it with the unerring accuracy of salmon returning to the river of their birth.

I remember my grandmother, Baba (that's grandmother in Yiddish), standing in the middle of a butcher shop on Jerome Avenue in the Bronx, spreading the feathers on the chicken in front of her and sniffing the skin to see if it was fresh—*in three or four places!* The butcher finally snapped, "Lady, do you think *you* could pass a test like that?" She just kept sniffing. That woman had a nose for what was real. And while I didn't recognize it then, she was one of my earliest teachers in how to sense truth without needing it explained.

There is within each of us that perfect guidance system. In most of us, it is simply a bit rusty from lack of use. The mechanism exists, and all we have to do to put it into shape is to use it.

CHAPTER FOUR

Cleaning Up the Gears

I GREW UP IN THE BRONX, very far away from the kinds of thoughts and questions I am expressing. What was important were very physical things like food, shelter, stickball, and making sure no one thought I was a "patsy" who could be pushed around. My family handled the food and shelter while I handled the rest by learning the rules inherent in growing up in the Bronx. For example, I periodically wound up in fights until I joined the football team in my very tough high school. When I wore the Jacket or Sweater with my varsity letter, everyone knew I had about 15 brothers. The result? No fights.

It wasn't just the fights or the stickball or the high school turf rules that shaped me—it was Baba's mysterious ability to erase my bad decisions with an act of love that looked to me like sabotage. Like the time she found out I was riding my new bike in traffic and—poof—the bike disappeared. That's the kind of love that leaves a mark.

As I grew, I naturally looked for the rules inherent in my environment. Looking back, it felt like I'd been running my life on autopilot—like the gears were grinding beneath the surface, filled with old habits and unexamined beliefs. I didn't know it then, but I was overdue for a serious tune-up, a serious cleaning of the gears. What I found when I began to wake up in my consciousness was that I had left a wide swath of garbage behind me. There was unfinished business everywhere. What's worse, I could see that unless I changed the way I was acting, speaking and even thinking, I would continue to pollute the world with my own particular brand of debris. When I first realized the real beauty of creation, I knew I had to cut that stuff out. It took years.

Cutting it out meant first becoming aware and then changing the way I was relating to the world and myself. Second, it meant wanting to change. Third, it required that I develop an awareness of the way I was actually acting in the world. Fourth, it meant I had to have some understanding that there was a different way of being in the world that was available to me. I had to learn the rules of this environment. Finally, it meant that I had to simply take myself in my own two hands, knowing that no one was going to do it for me, and change. It is a continuing, in fact never-ending, process.

By the way, I am not saying that this is the only way to accomplish this kind of thing. It is not. The paths are as diverse as humanity itself. It just happens to be the path I have taken, and so the only one I can talk about.

All of this is what I meant by cleaning up the gears.

I found that we have set up patterns for our speech, thoughts, and actions. We function on automatic pilot by simply following these patterns as long as they work. Becoming conscious means no more than becoming aware of these patterns so we can decide, as a matter of our own free will, whether we really want to continue to react to someone yelling at us in the way we did when we were three years old. We are free to choose once we know we have a choice and we know what the choices are. It is in manifesting this freedom to choose that real power exists.

What brings us to the point where we sincerely want to change? In a word, pain. If it sometimes seems that the world is conspiring against you to make you downright miserable, it may be because it is. Creation has clear, unyielding rules. If we live in such a way that violates these rules, we feel pain. It is no more complicated than that. Pain serves two functions. The most important is as a warning to us. Pain tells us when we are digressing from the rules and forces us back into line or else. At some point, we have all said, or will say, "Okay, I give up, I can't stand this anymore. There must be something else to life. Please show me." As we sincerely ask that question, we have taken the first step to freedom. Once we ask, it is in the nature of creation that the answers are provided to us just as quickly as we can absorb them. Again, this is one of the rules of the road. The universe has been created along very definite lines. One of the rules is that anyone who asks a question sincerely is given the answer. Try it, it works. All you have to do is pay close attention and be willing to accept the answer that is given to you. **Even if it is not the one you thought it was going to be.** After all, if you knew the answer to the question in advance, you were asking the wrong question.

I mentioned two reasons for pain. The second involves what is loosely called karma. Karma is really nothing more than one corollary for a very basic law, the law of balance. In the beginning, All was perfectly balanced; that is the nature of All. It can be nothing but perfectly balanced. Since we can say that, when we look over what we call time, certain imbalances appear to have occurred, there must be some mechanism for restoring each particular kind of imbalance, because in the end, when All That Is merges, it must again be balanced. Karma is the mechanism. It is simply that process which restores the balance. For every pain caused, balance requires that the same pain be suffered. For every harsh word given, balance requires that one be received. For every kindness performed, balance requires that a kindness be granted. There is no such thing as "good" or "bad" karma. Karma does not differentiate in that way. It is a law. It does not evaluate. It just operates to restore harmony in the universe. It is inexorable. The balance must be restored, either by the one who created the imbalance, or by one who is willing and is allowed to transfer sufficient previously earned credits to recreate the balance without the suffering it might otherwise entail. This is what we call grace.

All of this goes to explain the mechanisms designed to bring us back to Truth. Just as we learn as small children to avoid flames because they bring us pain, so do we also learn to avoid violating the rules of the universe because doing so brings us suffering. Unfortunately, we tend to learn the latter much more slowly than the former. At some point, however thick we have chosen to be, we get the message, and then true learning can begin in earnest.

CHAPTER FIVE

Receptivity

I HAVE FOUND THAT IT TAKES YEARS to clear the underbrush away so that sunlight can nourish the tender sprouts of young dedication to Truth. Each unthinking habit chokes Truth. Each careless phrase denies creation. Clearing away this underbrush is a prerequisite to any real growth. There is no particular reason that it should take years to accomplish; in theory, it can be done instantly. In fact, however, we are all more or less attached to our insanities.

We indulge our idiosyncrasies, encourage the foolishness of our friends and, in one way or another, distrust those who do not, or are "too good." In short, we have all been accustomed to our ways, and we have been too lazy and/or too afraid to change them. For those who decide to change them, what is usually necessary is time and help. And I had help.

In retrospect, my earliest teacher was my grandmother, whom we called Baba. Had it not been for Baba's extraordinary courage and foresight, my Jewish family and at least one young, orphaned girl whom she had taken in would not have survived the war and found their way to safety. Just before World War II, Baba saw the writing on the wall in Poland and got my family out just before the Nazis came in. Almost all of her eight brothers and sisters stayed and were killed. Over seven years, her decisions took the family from Poland to Russia, Siberia to Central Asia, then to postwar Germany, and finally across the ocean to Ellis Island. We settled in the Bronx, where we had relatives. Baba ran the household while my father, grandfather and mother worked. Baba cooked and baked everything from scratch—in abundance! She made sure we would never know the hunger they had known too well during the war. Throughout her life, Baba imparted her wisdom, frequently through Yiddish songs. There was one which, loosely translated, meant "Don't think of the past, it's gone. Don't think of the future, it's just a dream. Act in the present." It sounded much better sung in Yiddish.

Baba showed respect for Jewish traditions every Friday by lighting the candles and reciting her prayer. And yet, when I heard about the coming of the Messiah in Hebrew school and asked her when the Messiah would arrive, she replied, "If he were crawling on his belly like a snake, he would have been here by now." My father, whose father was a rabbi, was beside himself. Baba's humor, respect, and, above all, love supported the best in me.

I never stop telling Baba stories when I lead the meditation group. The group even bought her a chair so she could sit with us in comfort.

My first spiritual teacher was **David Pomerantz**. I met him at a party in the mid-70's. He invited me to dance with him. We were both terrible dancers. He told me he was teaching about chakras, and I wound up in his heart chakra class. That was the beginning of a more than forty-five year friendship. David introduced me to Hilda and remained my best friend until he passed. His groups on both coasts still meet, led by his wife Amalya. His seminars and books, mostly about Hilda, have touched thousands.

My most profound experiences came from my contact with **Hilda Charlton**. Hilda was beyond words. I was in her living room any number of times when people called with emergencies. As she and all who were present prayed for them, they stopped bleeding, and their pain and/or coughing disappeared. She rarely showed off her power in public, but on one occasion at her class at Synod House in the Cathedral of St. John the Divine in New York City, she stopped for a moment, looked out at the audience and said, "Raise your hand if you don't believe energy is real." About a dozen skeptics raised their hands.

She called them onstage, lined them up, and stationed one of her bigger students behind each person like a human catcher's mitt. Then she walked in front of the line, hand outstretched and palm out, but *not touching anyone.*

And one by one, they fell backwards. Not fainting. Just—gently toppling over backwards, like dominoes with dignity, each one caught by the student behind them.

Nobody said a word. You just knew: Something had happened.

One day, Hilda told me I needed to start a meditation group. She didn't ask; she told me. I responded that I had never run a meditation group, but she said, pointing to David Pomerantz, who was right next to me, "David will help you." He never did. I just did what seemed appropriate at the time and, starting with two people, more people came and kept coming. For forty-six years! Whenever someone thanked me, I always thanked them for coming. I have always felt that I learned as much from the group as they did from me. It just seems to me that teaching something makes it real in a way it was not before. It has been wonderful for me.

I believe we learn at three levels:

We learn with our minds, we learn with our feelings—and then the deepest part of us puts it all together. For me, teaching clarifies and consolidates what I have experienced. And so it has been with the meditation group. I have led the group for decades. While I have been teaching them how to meditate, they have been teaching me how to live.

My experiences with teaching and teachers, including Hilda and David Pomerantz, were based on meditation. My daughter, Staci Boden, put me in touch with a different healing path. Staci brings her own medicine, her own questions, her own fierce integrity. And her love shows up in forms I never imagined. She connects Earth-based wisdom with everyday living. Her book, *Turning Dead Ends into Doorways,* is an empowering guide for navigating life's challenges with practical spirituality. Watching her become who she is has made me very proud. Currently, her services through Dancing-Tree emphasize somatic coaching, energy healing and dance ceremony. I'm grateful for her, not just as a father, but as a fellow traveler.

As the title of this chapter brings to the fore, receptivity to what is happening externally and within is crucial for growth. I have learned that nothing happens unless you open to the possibility of it. As I opened inside over the years, some very unusual and wonderful things came our way. Early on, as attendance at the Tuesday evening meditations became more regular for more people, I thought it would be nice to have a place to meet for retreats. I looked in the Grass Valley/Nevada City area of California because it was highly wooded, beautiful and tranquil. But everything was expensive, and we had no money. And then, one Tuesday, **Sarah** showed up with her friend **Richard**. As he got to know us, he volunteered to give us some property he owned outside of Grass Valley. It had a small cabin on it that we could use for retreats. He called it, according to the sign outside the door, "Richard's Raunchy Ranch." One of us, **Rick**, was an excellent contractor. He and I went to look at it. The location, next to the national forest on just under an acre of land, was perfect, but Richard's cabin was a disaster. We asked him if we could tear it down and build something new. Without hesitating, he said, "Sure, and I would be glad to help." And so we did. Working on Saturdays, it took all who wished to participate from the meditation group about a year and a half to build what we wanted. With Rick's expert guidance, we tore down the old cabin, poured a new foundation and built a lovely two-story cabin. Richard's Raunchy Ranch transformed into our meditation retreat. For about thirty years, we and others, including David Pomerantz, used it for retreats, and sometimes people simply went there to meditate. Richard and Rick were as kind as they were generous. We became close friends.

By the time we got the land, I had a formative experience that greatly opened me. I was in my late twenties. I refer to it as my "**awakening experience.**" While I don't try to force things into my life, I find that, when I am open to something, the occurrences come more frequently.

It all started with a yoga retreat held near San Francisco, led by an American disciple of some Sri-Somebody. He called himself a yogi. I went. There were probably fifty people at the retreat.

The idea was to go *beyond the mind* by exhausting its ability to invent things. I partnered with just about everyone there, one at a time. The core question was "Who am I?" Working in pairs, we answered with whatever came up. Friday night to Sunday night, we did this. Every twenty minutes, a new partner. No reactions allowed. Just open space. Periodically, I'd look around. People were having experiences and going up to the teacher to validate them.

I got nothing. Over and over again—nothing. And our leader said, "Let's add one more exercise. Pick your partner." So there it was, I had one more opportunity to have an experience of who I was. One person who reached out to me to partner was someone I felt intuitively I should not work with, but there he was, so I said yes, and we worked as a pair for the last round.

Again, NOTHING happened. It was time to go. I had been attracted to one of the other participants and asked her if she needed a ride to San Francisco. She said she had one, and immediately behind her was the man I had worked with for the last two rounds. He heard the conversation and shared that he was from San Francisco and needed a ride. I felt I could not say no, so the two of us set off to the city together. As we started to get close to the city, I asked him where he wanted to be dropped. He replied that he had no place to sleep and asked if I could put him up for the night.

I had a two-bedroom Victorian flat. I gave him the spare room. As for me, I still slept in the nude back then. I took off my clothes, crawled into bed, and called it a night.

The day had seemed useless to me, even annoying, but I was staying open.

Middle of the night—I sat bolt upright in bed. It was how I imagine it feels to be struck by lightning, except not painful. I had **absolute certainty that the words that came to mind with the lightning strike—"I am what I experience"—were true. But I had no one to share them with who might validate my experience, except the person in the other bedroom.**

I ran naked into my guest's room and said, "Can I tell you what I just realized about myself?" He nodded. I gave him the full download. He looked at me like I was crazy.

I was in a euphoric state. I'd finally experienced something meaningful to me and asked, "What do you think?" looking for affirmation.

He shrugged. "I don't know. I'm just a guy."

The next day, I went to the office as usual in my three-piece suit with my briefcase. The feeling of the experience was still with me, and it felt really good. I called the retreat leader and told him what had happened. He said it sounded real.

That was my first real awakening experience. It blew me open. It was my deepest experience of Truth. "I am what I experience." From then on, I did what I could to be aware of what I felt in the moment.

Later, at a second retreat with the same teacher, I was walking up every five minutes to tell him about my experiences. That first one had opened the floodgates.

Now that I had what I considered my first experience of Truth, I was so earnest in my sincerity that I was downright obnoxious. I had tasted what I considered to be Truth, and it had gone directly to my head. I was out to explain it all to anyone who would listen. After all, it was now all so clear to me.

One day, for instance, I decided I wanted to share my new state of being with people. So, I sat in the first row of a public bus, directly behind the bus fare box. People had to bend over to insert their fare into the box, and when straightening up to go to a seat, they just had to look at me. I saw that as my opportunity. I eagerly tried to make eye contact with every individual who came on the bus to share the love that I felt inside. Not a single person even looked at me. In retrospect, I suspect that I was lucky they did not simply have me hauled away. As David Pomerantz said to me, "There was a time period you were hard to be around."

It took much more time for me to understand that my way was not the only way, that people had to be given the opportunity to ask their own questions and find their own way. I eventually (although not quickly enough for most of my friends) dropped my "True

Believer" approach to the path and began to focus upon correcting only what I wished to change in myself. I had concluded that I could only contribute to the world that which I could find in myself. For me, this was the beginning of sincere receptivity to learning.

From the perspective of sincere receptivity, the world is constantly providing guidance. It constantly touches the places within that are sensitive and exposes them. In this way, the world makes us strong. Of course, the nature of creation is such that it performs this service for all beings always. The only difference is that the rate of learning is immeasurably increased when the student understands that this is a great gift and the universe is not a matter of happenstance and not "out to get him."

It is for the student to accept this gift with the understanding that the "slings and arrows of outrageous fortune…" are not personal attacks. The universe is just set up this way. When we cease believing in the malevolence of the universe, we acquire the possibility of seeing its perfection. It is the vision of this perfection that can truly bring us to God.

I would like to add that I also discovered that Truth has a sense of humor. A few weeks after the bus lesson, I was walking through Macy's at Christmastime—one of my least favorite places at any time—when I was suddenly swept up by a wave of bliss and gratitude. I stopped and said, out loud, "Thank you." That, too, was receptivity.

Photo Gallery

David's daughter Staci is a somatic coach, spiritual teacher, and author. David is deeply proud of her and her work.

26 | FROM THE NOTEBOOK *of a* NEW YORKER

Here, David Pomerantz exudes happiness along with his wife, Amalya Pomerantz, who is carrying on the leadership of Gracelight since David Pomerantz's passing in 2024. She was his dedicated spiritual partner and support for 34 ½ years.

David Pomerantz (right) was David's best friend and teacher, as well as the leader of Gracelight, a beautiful spiritual community. David Rotman is on the left.

Here, David enjoys time with Rick (left), the first member of his meditation group and a building contractor. Rick led the meditation group in building the retreat house, from planning through hammering to completion. He was one of David's closest friends until he passed in 2000.

Photo Gallery | 29

Here, David works with Richard (right), who donated his property in the mountains, helped build the retreat house on the land, and became a dedicated group member as well as one of David's best friends. He passed in 2017.

This is the house the group built; it hosted weekend retreats for decades. Its vibration was heavenly.

Maria understands work. Maria understands commitment. Her help was invaluable in building the retreat house, and her contact with David has continued to be a source of support for him.

Some participants at this meditation retreat gathered in the upstairs meditation room, beaming the love that everyone was feeling.

Photo Gallery | 31

Members of the meditation group paused in front of the retreat house during a work weekend. You can feel the group spirit.

A number of precious children grew up as part of the meditation group family, and absorbed the joy.

David shared a happy moment with Jahnavi at Rick and Wendy's wedding. Jahnavi is his dear friend who supported his work, coordinated group gatherings, and infused all communications with love for many years.

As group members moved out of the San Francisco Bay area, David began leading weekly meditations via Zoom. LB (left) and Linda (right) are two of the members who lead meditations when David is not available. Linda was member #3 in the group. By filling in for David over the years, especially when his mediations ran late, she kept the group together. In recent years, Janis (middle) has taken over the group coordination and communications role from Jahnavi.

When Anouk first joined the meditation group, she brought 108 questions (just on day one!) David humored her. Over time, she let go of the need to "figure it all out," and instead relaxed into the Ground of Being—and her heart. A couple of decades later, she teaches meditation and supports leaders through trauma-informed somatic coaching. She played a pivotal role in bringing this book into the world.

Kathy (left, shown with Linda) is the one who always steps forward when something needs to be done. David found that it's much easier to start a book than to finish it. Kathy, Janis, and Anouk provided the energy necessary to finish it.

One of our love stories: Rick and Wendy met through the meditation group, fell in love, married, and have a wonderful son, Austin. Wendy has held the energy and supported the unity of the group ever since.

CHAPTER SIX

The Unfolding Vision

When we have cleared away the underbrush of our old habits and have made ourselves receptive to the physical world's feedback on a moment-to-moment basis, we can live by principles that much more accurately reflect the deeper laws of creation, and so we find that life has become increasingly kind to us. In fact, life becomes downright pleasant. Most of the pain is gone.

It now becomes necessary, really essential, that control of the process of unfolding be taken away from the mind. The mind is humanity's greatest tool. It forges creation. It is the medium through which the higher realities express themselves in the physical world. Yet with all that the mind is, it is merely a tool for the use of the higher self. It cannot be allowed to control, only to carry out the orders of that inner voice, which the student is coming to know and accept. In essence, the mind is a very sophisticated reasoning mechanism, a computer, which must be brought firmly under the control of that within you which is becoming increasingly receptive to Truth.

At this point, it starts to become increasingly clear that the mind frequently doesn't know what to do, and that those simple truths inside, which we have given time to grow, start to seem relevant. Those simple truths that we have been nurturing are not from the mind, they are feelings, which come increasingly from the deepest part of us, and, as we work with them, we learn, increasingly, that following them gives us much that we cannot have by following the mind.

I mentioned earlier that my deepest experience of Truth is that I am what I experience. It's my experiences that forge Truth. That is not to say that words do not form Truth. Mind has no concept of that which it cannot understand. It is not that Truth is irrational, it is simply beyond the experience of the mind, and the mind cannot lead you all the way to it. So we must look somewhere else for guidance.

Words, thoughts and deeds all form this world, but it is the pure experience that gives us the truest feeling for what is really going on. If we rely less on feelings and more on words, the very vocabulary that we use will limit what we can communicate to ourselves and others. At some point, only experience will convey your truth to you. I tell my meditation group, not infrequently, to ignore what I say completely, to *just feel it*. In fact, I give them feedback on how well they have ignored what I said, and I instead focus on what is inside them. It's easy for me to see whether they have stayed with their inner feelings, because being with them when they stay with their inner feelings is very different than being with them when they stay in their thoughts. It takes a little while, but after a while, they get it. The stronger feeling derives from their experience, not the words.

As we make the transition from being directed by the mind, we develop a sense of something inside us that is much wiser and more powerful. Only you have within you your personal directions to The All, and they take the form of the feelings within you that you have learned to trust over time.

That which can take you the entire way starts with your increasing appreciation and trust in that small voice within you that expresses itself when you are still. That is the voice of Truth, of Perfection. We can only refuse to allow our minds to make our decisions when we see the perfection within us and increasingly trust that which we feel is the voice of that perfection. By focusing on that perfection with the confidence that perfection is humanity's true state, we begin to have increasing confidence in that voice within. We begin to rely on it in small and then in increasingly more significant matters. Please notice, I said "confidence," not "faith." Please don't misunderstand. I am not downgrading faith. It's okay. It has worked very well as a basis for action for thousands of years. For me, however, "confidence" implies a degree of appreciation for the laws of creation that is not implicit in "faith." Faith does not require understanding. Confidence is built on faith, but goes beyond in expressing an appreciation for the laws of creation and acting with a faith and understanding of what the results of each action will be.

At this point, the seeker has taken a substantial journey, but the most important parts still remain.

CHAPTER SEVEN

LEARNING THE LESSONS

Outlining the general contours of the path we follow is easy when compared with walking that path. What is clear and comprehensible in the abstract becomes muddled in the reality of day-to-day life. As I have gone through my own lessons, I have found that certain attitudes or states of mind are most helpful in making this journey with a minimum of confusion. They are patience, forgiveness, gratitude and positivity. Each of these is really an approach to seeing the world. When we train ourselves to respond to any situation with a combination of these perspectives, the result will be more balance and equilibrium in our daily lives.

Patience

Of all of these, patience is probably the most difficult to learn. We have very few models for it in our culture. We tend to think of life as something that just happens, so waiting for the "happening" can be difficult. If we think of life as unfolding, we begin to appreciate that each moment is connected to the prior and next one, and we begin to understand why patience is important. It is not only important to experience each moment, but to experience it in the context of its antecedent and subsequent moments. Context affects the meaning of the moment and patience is necessary to integrate context.

I saw this lesson in my work as a mediator. Sometimes the best thing I could do was hold silence a few seconds longer than felt comfortable. Let the storm pass. Let someone breathe. Patience isn't passive. It's active stillness.

We tend to seek immediate gratification for all of our wants. The speed of our lives is often so great that we take it for granted that everything happens quickly. Yet, it does not. Everything has a perfect time and place. Creation expresses itself differently in different times and places. Each form of expression must be allowed to ripen by itself before it can become manifest. We cannot hurry the process. By picking the fruit too soon, we will never be able to enjoy its sweetness. Patience is the essential prerequisite to timing. We must learn to wait until our inner voice says, "Go."

The notion of patience is really simply the expression of respect for the process by which life is unfolding around us. When we respect that process, we do not seek to hurry or change it. We simply watch for the appropriate moment to sound our notes in the massive symphony of life. This does not mean that we have to wait and do nothing. The orchestra is always playing. There are always notes we can play. We just have to accept the fact that the notes our personality may wish to play in any given moment are completely out of touch with the rest of the orchestra. It would be disastrous to attempt to play those notes. When we play the notes that fit, they provide a sound magnified thousands of times by the rest of the orchestra. That is real power. It is worth paying attention for those moments.

Forgiveness

Forgiveness is another matter. We usually think of forgiveness as some arcane virtue divorced from our reality and generally within the province of some sort of priest, or of God alone. We may seek forgiveness from someone, or we may forgive someone, but we do not tend to think in terms of forgiving ourselves. This is nonsense. The fact is that we are evolving creatures who are often wrong and misguided. We may make a lot of mistakes, perhaps even the same mistakes over and over (and over and over) again, but we *must* forgive ourselves for making these mistakes. It is for us to forgive ourselves before God can forgive us. Quite frankly, I don't think that God really cares all that much about whether we didn't get the job we wanted, or whether we passed that test we just took. It is not that God doesn't care about us or isn't keeping track of what is going on around here. It is simply that there is already a mechanism set up in the world that will force any imbalance we have created to redress itself.

Karma. God doesn't have to worry about it all, it is an automatic process. Now, if God doesn't have to worry about it, why should you?

I am not saying that we should be indifferent to the consequences of our actions, or use all of this as an excuse to do anything we wish, regardless of whether it hurts others. I am just saying that there is no need to feel guilty about the mistakes we make. Guilt helps no one, least of all ourselves. Guilt ties up our energy so completely that further movement becomes impossible. Guilt stops learning. It prevents further evolution. Don't get caught in it. Forgive yourself. Whatever you do, forgive yourself and, at the same time, try to do better next time around. The goal is to do the best you can do. Keep your eyes on the goal and keep going for it. Do not detour. Remember that you do not have to punish yourself. Karma will automatically take care of that for you. You can cheerfully go forward in gratitude, knowing that, at some point, you will have to accept the consequences for every misdeed. There is no need to feel guilty about it. The system is set up so that we must pay. It is not necessary for us to keep track of the bill. That is done with unerring accuracy. Now, doesn't that just brighten your whole day?

Gratitude

Given this apparently ever-increasing debt, you might well ask, "What is there to be grateful about?" Actually, the fact that karma exists is one of the reasons to be grateful, but it goes far beyond that. The world has been created to maximize our opportunities for learning. The world is perfect. It was created in perfection. Each of the rules that govern its operation functions perfectly. I can't prove this to you through reason. I simply ask that you hold it as a possibility and test this possibility against your continuing experiences about life and decide for yourself. If it were not so, then chaos would result. I do not see chaos at the heart of the universe; I see order. In fact, all around me I see order. The geometric perfection of the shape of each snowflake, the precision with which a bird builds its nest and the beauty and order of a symphony which touches my heart all clearly reflect that perception. I believe that, if we look for the beauty and order in all of life, we will always find it. If we look for the chaos, we will find that. I am eternally grateful for the fact of perfection, beauty, truth and, most of all, love in the universe. I know that everything each of us is going through will give rise to the perfect expression of God. I know this from deep inside myself. I have no doubt of it at all. I do not ask you to share that certainty (although you are free to share it without my asking), but only to find those things in the world for which you are grateful and think of them when things get difficult. Focusing always on the positive is a fine way to minimize our detours from the path.

We can even be grateful for each of the bumps we hit each day. Each time we react negatively, get lost, blow up, or in some way act inconsistently with our highest understandings, we are expressing something within us that is not quite clear yet. Instead of being upset, allow yourself to feel grateful for the lesson you have just learned. Forgive yourself for making the mistake and move on to do better next time. That is all you need to do.

Positivity

All of this brings me to an essential ingredient underlying all the others: positivity. Nothing can be accomplished without positivity. Whether focused through learning, love, devotion or action, positivity is essential. There was a time when I made small buttons, which my friends could pin to their clothing. The buttons said, "No need to be pessimistic. It wouldn't work anyway." You can get lots of smiles by expressing an obvious truth.

My own positivity arises from the certainty within me that life has a direction, and that direction is ever upward and back to God. I know in myself that Love is the essence of life, and we are all its expression. Given all of that, how could life and each action in it be anything but positive? Again, I do not ask you to accept my views. Each of us must come to our own understandings and express them in our own way. I ask only that you suspend your disbelief and try being positive. Train yourself to see the appropriateness of each event. When something happens that looks terrible, look for the good and rightness in it. Train yourself always to see a half glass of water as half full rather than as half empty.

Positivity is an attitude of the mind. The Western mind has been trained to be critical, to analyze and search for faults. There is nothing wrong with such training. I do not ask that you disregard it, but only that when you use it you come back to the perspective that whatever you see as faults or problems are merely temporary, created to allow you to test yourself, to learn and grow. Remember your direction is always up. That is truly positive. Do not focus on the weeds as you pull them, but on the beauty of the garden (and the beauty within each weed). Positivity is the key to all progress. It slowly grows within us as we develop the certainty that life is not chaotic but perfect, and that we have our perfect parts to play in it. Nurture positivity within you, so that it may speed your return home.

CHAPTER EIGHT

The Mechanisms of Release

I have already spoken at length of the general outlines of the evolutionary path we are all following. Much more, however, can be said about the specific process that we follow. The guideposts along the path should become familiar. Just as there are certain states of mind which are of real assistance in this journey, so there are also certain shortcuts one may take to deal with particular situations. These are really just tricks that we can train ourselves to use.

The first and most important is laughter. It is impossible to stay depressed when we laugh. The whole formation of a laugh makes it impossible to do anything but brighten up. People have been writing and speaking of the power of laughter for eternity, but it is still not widely understood. Laughter does something at each level of existence. Everything from the physical body and up benefits. If we could train ourselves to laugh in any situation, especially the ones that really look bad, it would brighten our entire path and considerably lighten our load. It is also healthy and nutritious, but I warn you, it is addictive. Laughing will instantly raise your spirits and bring you the goodwill of those around you. Laugh as best you can. If you don't really mean it at first, don't worry, just laugh anyway, and in a short time, you will begin to laugh from the heart. Laughter just has incredible power to bring joy and positivity. Pay attention to how much you laugh and be sure to get your quota in each day.

One of the reasons that laughter probably works is that it forces us to breathe. The only real breaths that many people take are when they laugh. We tend to breathe very shallowly, and as things get more difficult or we get more depressed, our breath becomes increasingly restricted. It should come as no surprise to you that breath is vital to life. It should also come as no surprise that making certain we at least periodically take full breaths and exhale fully is essential to staying positive and growing. There are many breath exercise techniques available. Sometimes it may be best to breathe in a slow, steady way seeking smoothness; sometimes deep full breaths are much more appropriate. I am not advocating any particular technique, or even that you do any technique at all. What is most important for most of us is simply that we pay attention to those times when we are simply not breathing, and start. When unhappy, breathe. When not feeling well, breathe. When afraid, breathe. All it takes initially is paying attention to those times when we are not allowing ourselves to get air. Breathing will release you.

At certain times in our development, breath exercises may be a significant way to speed our individual growth. They can be very powerful. In fact, they can give the student access to more power than the student may be capable of dealing with. To my mind, there are too many breath techniques available with too little emphasis being given on guiding the student's overall development so that he or she does not overload on the immense source of power that these techniques can open up. In short, please be careful and go slowly. If you are doing systematic breath exercises, make sure you have competent supervision.

All of these are really only tricks. Of course they work, because they are consistent with the basic Laws of Creation at the heart of this reality, but there is no real need to understand the specifics of why they work, only that they do. Use them.

Perhaps the most powerful of all the "tricks" I have picked up so far is the simple one of "letting go." This is difficult to understand because it is contrary to what most people have been taught about what they must go through to change or feel better. My own premise in life is that the heart of All is perfect and Perfection is within us at all times. From that, it seems clear to me that any deviation from perfection, any disharmony or unhappiness or dis-ease, is the result of our imposing a layer of one sort or another on our basic perfection. These things arise only because we have placed something between the "I" that we are in touch with and our true selves. All we have to do is let that "something" go. That is all. We do not have to analyze it, trace its history back to our early childhood problems with our parents, or to the way we died in a prior incarnation. In fact, we do not even have to know what the specific layer was. To let go of it just requires letting go of it.

Whenever I tell people this, someone always asks, "But, how do you let go?" It appears they want detailed instructions on the mechanics of it, but who gave us detailed instructions on how to walk? We just got up and did it, keeping our intention on doing it and then just keeping at it. Learning to let go is precisely the same. At first, we may require some kind of permission from a therapist, a friend or ourselves to let go. Sometimes we require the permission of our minds, and we refuse to let go until we "understand" what happened. Sometimes we will not let go until we feel a priest or God or ourselves has forgiven us. While one or more of these things may be necessary for any particular individual to forgive himself or herself in a given situation, it is only necessary because that person has made it a condition of release. There are no inherent conditions of release. God holds no grudges. Your mind cannot bar your progress by seeking lengthy explanations if you do not allow it to do so. You really can simply let go of whatever comes up without engaging in a long process of seeking permission. In fact, the natural process of evolution within us brings us continually closer to the point where we are constantly letting go instantaneously of everything that comes between our true self and the expression of that self. Those who have mastered this have mostly mastered themselves and the world.

I do not ask that you accept all of this, or any of this, right now. For now, simply accept the possibility that it is true and allow yourself to move in this direction. We all learned to crawl, walk and run. I believe we can move much faster than that.

At family weekends at the retreat house, children showed us how to laugh and let go. Here, Javier is enjoying the tree swing.

CHAPTER NINE

Our Immediate Needs

We have all learned from the time we were very small that to take care of our needs, we had to go through certain steps. To seek, to ask, to demand, to reason, to cry, to cajole and many more were the ways we experimented in order to achieve what we desired. We slowly built up patterns of responding to given situations in particular ways that we had learned would be effective. When a particular response worked, we continued to repeat it, and it became more automatic. In this way, we developed the mechanisms to fulfill whatever we considered to be our immediate needs. Almost all of us continue to follow these same patterns for as long as they work to provide us with what we consider to be important. Many of us go no further than continuing to respond to the same need with variations of the same patterns.

In short, we become stimulus-response automatons to varying degrees, as long as what we do works to satisfy our "needs" and brings us a degree of whatever we define as "happiness" or "fulfillment." It usually takes a shock of some sort, some kind of pain, some situation where "the usual solution" doesn't work, for us to begin to discover the extent to which we really have been functioning on "automatic." When I found out how little of what I was doing really made a difference to me, I was shocked, and at the same time amazed that I had seen so little for so long.

It is not necessary to wait until pain brings us to our knees seeking a better way. What can we do now to understand our needs and our ways of filling them? There are simple questions that you may ask now about yourself and your way of expressing yourself in the world.

Look around your world. Are you always looking towards some kind of reward from someone or something in the world? Does your own happiness, your own feelings of joy, elation, sorrow, wholeness, and, most of all, of being loved depend on the feedback you get from someone else?

If these are your "wants," you are, in one fashion or another trying, by whatever you have learned works for you, to satisfy them. Some of us have learned to satisfy these needs by being nice, others by being difficult. Some of us learned to work hard to satisfy these needs. Others have learned to rely on what they call "luck." Some of us have learned to demand what we seek; others to wait.

These are all the same. All we are doing in each of these situations is making our own happiness depend on something, which we assume is outside of us. As long as we assume anything is outside of us, we have based our actions on a fallacy. As long as we seek to satisfy ourselves by satisfying some condition of the world or of someone in it, we are misdirecting our energy and denying our own power. Yet we all do this! Why?

In truth, we do this out of a lack of understanding of who we really are. We may intellectually believe we are all one and all God, but when it comes right down to it, when we need a new apartment, we will go through the steps we have always followed (plus or minus current suggestions from our friends) to find it. Our belief is rather shallow.

Yet that shallow belief, or even the belief that there may be another way, can be nurtured into a maturity that can stagger the world with its power. I had a client with a very large parking lot, which always filled up before I got there at about noon. It took me forever to find a space until I changed the paradigm I was using. I felt that if I looked long enough, I would find a space, and I did, but it sometimes took quite of bit of looking.

It finally occurred to me that I might just as easily assume I could, in some sense, "feel" where empty parking spaces were. I had nothing to lose and could always go back to my first strategy, so I tried it. It took a while after I changed my paradigm, but the empty parking spots came much more quickly. Although parking lots at ski resorts when the snow is good are a particular challenge.

I never try to "manifest" by trying to use my mind to visualize what I want or otherwise force it into existence. That may work well for some people, but it takes a lot of work. I prefer to simply allow it to exist in my mind instead of focusing on the fact that it is not evident at the moment.

My nephew was staying with me, and we were skiing together. One day he noticed something strange to him and asked, "Uncle David, why is it you always find a good parking place?" I replied, "I am open to always finding one." It was the simple truth. These are very small and perhaps trivial instances, and I refer to them because, when you change your mindset about how particular things happen, the world has an opportunity to let them happen in a new way.

We can nurture new beliefs by small trustings. Small successes over time give us the confidence to keep growing and asserting our truth as possibilities in the world. Let me repeat, I never try to create them in the world by visualization, repetition or mantras. I just make sure I am open to their existence.

Begin with small matters. Begin from the assumption that all is within, and only seeks expression in the world. From that assumption, consciously ask, don't demand, that the perfect expression of what you seek may be manifest. Give it the opportunity to be.

Please understand that you may not be able to immediately, or ever, walk on water or move mountains. Each of us has come into this life with particular limitations imposed by the laws of karma, among other things. But we all have incredibly wide latitude within those laws, and even beyond them. Grace, for example, can change karma. When we know that which we seek is already within us, we have all that we require for its manifestation, but please be careful about getting lost in the feeling of power that may come from manifesting. For me, the goal is to find and express God, or Truth, within us. Manifesting everything you could ever wish for will not bring you one whit closer to God. Only Love will do that. Only Love will allow us to truly focus upon and appreciate God.

If we spend our time concentrating on obtaining that which we feel we need, then we are always focusing on feeding ourselves with material goods, possessions, people, love and respect instead of focusing on what we may give to the world.

To say this another way, please understand that the entire focus of our lives is frequently spent in meeting our needs. We are constantly searching for that which we perceive to be necessary for our happiness, health or safety. In this search we initially make the mistake of thinking that all of this is, in some sense, outside of us. Mistake number one. All of this is inside us and readily accessible.

Mistake number two is the more difficult one. In our search for gratification, we can completely lose that the essential focus of Love is on giving, not receiving. In always seeking to satisfy our desires, we are always taking from the universe. Our true way is to give to the universe, not to take. Only in giving are we really able to receive the abundance of the universe.

But how do we make the shift? Are there not things which we need, and properly so? Yes, of course we must all take care that we meet whatever standards of living we feel at the moment are important for us to maintain. Yet, we must bring our desires under control, or they will continue to grow, and nothing will satisfy us, ever. Take your focus away from what the world can give, one step at a time in each area of your life, and be free of your desires. It is only through this kind of freedom that real happiness may be achieved.

Only when you teach what is inside of you can you truly make it your own. Open yourself to teaching what is inside of you—but don't get attached to being the teacher. Share, then move on to something else.

CHAPTER TEN

STABILITY

ONE KEY TO LIFE IS STABILITY. When I was younger, I very much enjoyed the roller coaster at the amusement park. I enjoyed the ups and even the downs that love and life in general provided. It was all so exciting. It was always changing and always different. There was stimulation everywhere, but it was always the stimulation provided by the external world, by physical reality. I was using physical reality to bring excitement to me. I have since found that, if I let it, my inner reality will bring a very different kind of physical excitement to the physical world. This excitement is filled with a wonder and joy that I did not know existed in this world. The only catch is that it is very sensitive. It can be easily overshadowed by external creation. It can only surface in the quiet and stillness of a contemplative mind and physical environment. In short, it requires stability to be experienced.

The stability I speak of is not achieved by forcing a rigid structure upon the mind and reality. One cannot find it by regimenting oneself so much that the sparks of bliss have no place to enter. It cannot be found in the rigidity of a mindset that does not change and expand with the changes and expansions of the deepest parts of the human heart as it grows in understanding itself. This kind of rigidity will not create stability, for it is not built on Truth but only on a conception or some idea of truth. In such circumstances, Truth is being pushed into, forced into, a mold that will not quite fit. The result is instability.

The stability that I speak of is very different than this. It is based entirely on personal experience of Truth. Such personal experiences touch the core of creation. The seeker must find stability only in Truth, not in what he feels about Truth, or believes about Truth, but only *experiences* of Truth. But how is one to experience Truth, and then be sure it was Truth that was being experienced?

This is a short chapter because the first part of this question has already been discussed in Chapters 4 and 5. The answer to the second part is straightforward. When Spiritual Truth is experienced, it changes your life.

The first time I experienced Truth, I knew to a certainty that "I am what I experience." There was absolutely no doubt in me about it. It completely changed my life—instantaneously. I immediately lost all desire to eat meat and fish, my body changed dramatically, and I lost about twenty pounds within just a few weeks. I am not suggesting that everyone's experience of truth will be quite as dramatic as mine. I suppose I wanted the drama of the instantaneous shift, perhaps so I could write about it here. The essence of any contact with Truth, however, is the certainty of it. There really is no mistaking Truth, even though the mind attempts to cloud the experience, the experience remains bright and clear.

The other aspect of touching Truth, which has always been the same for me, is that it feels good. Sometimes it has brought me joy, at other times tears, but always, even when I cried tears of release, it felt good, or better than that, it felt wonderful. Truth really does bring happiness. I have never known it to be otherwise for myself or anyone else who has experienced it.

When we base our words, thoughts and deeds on Truth and Truth alone, we can create stability in our expression. That is really why stability is important. Stability is an essential prerequisite to pure expression, and after all, aren't we all here, not only to experience Truth, but to live it in the physical world?

This is what I consider to be true freedom: To be free at all times to express in our thoughts, words and deeds from the place of Truth. This is mastery, and it is this that brings lasting joy and bliss as inseparable companions. When we find the stability created by our understanding of the Truth within us, we have traveled a long way in our journey home.

CHAPTER ELEVEN

Rules of the Road

A. Driving

All of us have gone through the process of gaining permission to drive our cars. Many of us did this when we were young. In my case, my parents didn't drive. I had to go out and get driving lessons with money that I had saved doing odd jobs. Then, because I was very anxious to get out on the road and didn't want to wait until my 18th birthday, I got a special license in New York, which allowed me to drive only outside of New York City and then only during daylight hours. I was really anxious, so I got my license at 17 and bought my first car, a 1956 Chevy, for about $200.

My problem was that I lived in New York City, but about a mile from the Yonkers border. That didn't stop me, though. I would drive my car over the border and then feel the freedom of being able to drive legally wherever I wanted to outside the city. When I was done, I would return triumphantly to New York City, being very careful not to do anything that would cause me to be stopped by any police along the way. That one-mile stretch between the border and my home was no man's land. If I were stopped there, my precious driving privileges could be suspended or revoked, and my freedom would come to an end. I managed to do this for about two or three months between the time I got my license and my 18th birthday without incident so that, when I turned 18, I could triumphantly drive legally in New York City, no longer skulking to and from the border.

For me in all of this, learning to drive and taking the written test and the driving test was the easy part. Learning the rules that I was expected to follow on the road was not particularly difficult because it was a mental exercise. Learning physically how to drive the car was not particularly difficult because it was simply an exercise in mind and body coordination. What got difficult for me was applying all of that to my particular situation, living as I did a mile from the border. My theoretical knowledge of the rules of the road and my practical understanding of how to drive were useless unless I could practice, and I had to find my own way of doing that. And even when I began to practice, I knew it would take some period of time, perhaps months, perhaps years, before I became in any way proficient at driving, i.e., until the rules of the road and the coordination necessary to drive the car became automatic in me.

When I was young, it didn't occur to me to apply any of this to any spiritual lessons. I didn't even wake up at all until I was about 28. But it does make some sense now to think of it in this way. We can be taught the rules of the road either while in a body or between bodies. It is only when we are here on the earth that we can practice and actually make them our own, make them automatic. In my case, I was in such a hurry to begin that I wasn't willing to wait until I had the full permission of 18. I jumped the gun. In the same way, many of us come here as soon and as often as we can to practice that which we have come to understand but not yet fully made our own.

That for which we come, for which we take on a body, for which we suffer and eventually die, is no more complicated than this: We come to practice. We cannot practice in heaven because everything is instantly available there, so we all do the equivalent of going to Yonkers so we can practice until mastery finds us and we need practice no more. What is it we come to practice? We come to practice and make perfect the way in which we manifest our understanding of the universe, the nature of existence. In other words, our time here is simply for the purpose of learning how to express those basic rules, which form the first part of this small volume—or even more simply, to learn how to feel and express love.

It is quite easy to say simply, "These are the rules of life, follow them." The obvious response I've heard so often in myself and others is, "How?" That to me became the most difficult question. For me it was much easier to understand who I was than to be who I was.

How then do we make these rules our own? How do we live them? How on earth do we be who we are? If this were a serial drama, you would now have to wait until next week's installment, perhaps, to find answers to these questions. As it is, you can simply continue to the next chapter.

B. Once Over Lightly

It is said that "practice makes perfect." Obviously, the answer to the question of "How" is "Do." Obviously, what is necessary is practice. But, practice what? Before we discuss what, let's talk about how. How do we practice?

Volumes have been written talking at length about the prerequisites for the aspirant on the path. Hindu parables talk about the necessity of wanting God more than that single breath of air, which is the difference between life and drowning under water. We are told over and over again that only the serious aspirant, the one who is ready to die for their beliefs, can find the Truth. We are told the path is narrow and that only total dedication will keep us from falling off.

Yet how many of us start off on the path with total dedication? If we had total dedication from the start, we would be finished. If we wanted God now more than our very lives, we would have already realized God.

I spent years beating myself up about not being

serious enough before I realized that this approach assumed there was somewhere I wanted to go. When I realized that, a funny thing happened, I lightened up. That's when I stopped taking myself and that which I was doing quite so seriously. Then I found what has, to me, been an indispensable way of looking at this whole process. Lightly. With a smile in my heart, I found everything went much more smoothly.

You have to pick your God models. It's hard to imagine Jehovah smiling. He can be somebody else's God model. On the other hand, it's very easy for me to think of Jesus, Ramakrishna and even Buddha smiling a great deal. I have not known very many, but all the "god people" I have ever known loved to joke and laugh. And why not? If your perspective is the eternal, why should you get stuck in the foul-up of the last five minutes? And wouldn't it seem funny to someone whose perspective was the eternal to watch us get bogged down in worrying about how badly we had screwed up the last five minutes?

Once over lightly, television ads told us we do not have to scrub hard to take out the most stubborn stains when we have the proper product. Maybe the proper product here includes a degree of tolerance of our own missteps, or even love for that which is not perfect. Perhaps it's better to err on the light side rather than scrubbing until we've worked the shine off the tiles and the joy out of our lives.

C. Which Way?

So much for how to approach the path. But what about which path to choose? If anything on this subject becomes clear very quickly, it is that if you are seeking the infinite, the paths to it must also be of an infinite number. This will make immediate sense to someone living in San Francisco. We have an incredible variety of people and systems, all designed to lead somehow to Truth. How could it really be any other way? Since we all, each of us, are so different, how could we possibly conceive of a "one size fits all" path? So, perhaps the most significant feature of the path is its plurality.

When I really got into this stuff, I started in all different ways. There was "body work" and "diet" to clean out my bodily systems. There was hatha yoga for strengthening the body, pranayama for strengthening the nerves, meditation retreats for strengthening our connection with God, prayer, periodic fasting and of course service. Within each of these general subheadings, I, living in California, had a choice of dozens, if not hundreds, of people and types from which to choose. I had all this available, yet how does one choose? And, how do you know when you've chosen properly?

To me, the answers to these questions came as a result of several understandings. The first came as I was watching someone who was deadly earnest in taking at least fifty different kinds of supplements a day, in very specific proportions, in order to accomplish certain things for each organ of his body, his chakras and his connections with his higher self. He studied this matter quite carefully and formulated a very precise response to his needs. As I watched him going through his morning capsules, he asked why I hadn't done a similar thing. I said that I was not smart enough to figure all that out. He took me literally, but what he didn't really seem to understand was that he wasn't either. In fact, no one is that smart. The effect of all those supplements on each aspect of how we function is probably not fully understood by anyone, especially when you throw in the effects they have on each other. To know how fifty different kinds of anything will affect them and interact with each other is quite difficult. Even a simple breathing exercise may affect two different people in very, very different ways. Thus, we have very ancient and sage advice from masters on the one hand telling us not to eat fruit, and others telling us to eat nothing but fruit. (And similarly, providing advice on which fruits and vegetables to cook or not cook, and how to put it all together in meals.)

What I decided was, first of all, to go easy and not take all these choices so seriously. It just seemed to me that, whether or not I actually ever found Truth depended on what vitamins I took in what combination, first, I probably would never find it, and second, it was a darn silly system and I wasn't going to play in that ballgame. That's when things started making some sense. The key for me was when I realized I had a choice of games. You see, if there are an infinite number of ways to reach Truth, why can't I pick the ones that I want to participate in? In fact, if I believe it's the correct one, won't it, in fact, function as the correct one for as long as I hold that belief? Since reality exists only from our perspective to begin with, what's the problem with simply choosing what you want to do and how you want to do it?

I have heard the next question many times. "Aren't some paths better than others for me?" The answer to that is, of course. But that which is best is for you to decide for yourself.

Let me digress a moment. When I was going through all of this, it really seemed to me that I had to do everything properly—that there was a right mixture of things to do and a proper way of doing them. I was constantly judging myself by whether or not I had reached this standard of correctness of doing it right. Life is hard that way, folks. When we do that, we are constantly spending our time judging how we've done in the past rather than focusing on what's to be done in the present. There isn't much joy in a life that's spent constantly focused on grading yourself against a hypothetical perfection. That's really what it comes down to. Perfection is hypothetical. It doesn't exist here. To grade ourselves against it—to criticize ourselves for not reaching it would mean we're always seeing ourselves as having a shortfall. What's the alternative? Indeed, is there an alternative? You bet there is. Controlling your perspective. Let me explain.

D. Perspectives

Religions have dealt with this question of the possible paths to God in several ways. Some of them, in a very straightforward way that simply says, "This is the way—the only way. If you proceed by any other set of rules, follow any other path, you cannot find God." Other religions have recognized the multitude of paths and have tried to define them in such a way as to make some sense out of them. Traditional Hindu thought speaks of four major paths to the Lord: Bhakti or devotion, Jhana or wisdom, Siva or service, and Raja Yoga, which is a combination of specific tools designed to hasten the process. In addition, periodically, a master like Yogananda or Jesus will appear and give us a new system, or perhaps a subdivision of one of these four systems.

Perhaps, all these belief systems do is to lay out some routes across the desert so that we may not wander aimlessly through eternity, going in circles, following our own tracks and finally giving up or dying of thirst. Even so, they are still valuable, especially in the short term, to give meaning to a life. Or perhaps, giving up is not a bad choice to make, but then how else can we negotiate this way home—the way to Truth—without these or some guideposts? Without them, are we not doomed to wander aimlessly in the desert? I really don't think so; let me explain why.

First, I want to emphasize that these systems—virtually any system of rational thought and belief—will bring one close to Truth. What it will do depends solely on the perspective of the person who's using the system. As I've said before, the Old Testament version of God, the fire and brimstone variety that doesn't forgive or forget, that demands an eye for an eye, a tooth for a tooth, does not do much for me personally. Yet many people are drawn to these particular teachings because they fit what it is they came here to learn. They may, for example, be important in developing a strong sense of justice in an individual. These systems have value—but they have limits.

The funny thing is that the limits of these systems are really defined by the value they provide. If the value of the system is providing a sense of justice, then its limitation will be going beyond the sense of justice. Since justice is defined by the head and not the heart, there will frequently be occasions when the head will choose what the heart knows to be wrong. The head must have its learning, its understanding of justice, but at some point, it must learn to yield to the heart in particular situations. Perhaps the tragedy of King Arthur was that he could not make an exception for Guinevere and Lancelot because they did not fit his theoretical notion of justice, while in his heart, he knew that to condemn Guinevere to die because of her relationship with Lancelot was wrong.

But does this not make us rudderless once again? No, this does not mean we're rudderless. Instead, all of this emphasizes that our choice of direction, our choice of path, is a very individual one, which varies with circumstances in our own development. But if that is true, how do we answer the old question, the one we asked before, "How do we choose? How do we know we're right?" Having accepted the infinite diversity of routes to God, have we not, at the same time, made it impossible to proceed? The answer to that question could be that there are no right or wrong routes, just more or less appropriate ones, and living them will make it clear which are which. Or, perhaps there is an underlying current, an underlying stream that guides us. I know, at this point, this sounds very hypothetical, but perhaps I can make it a bit more real.

E. THE EARTH TURNS

Yes, I know you will all agree with this heading. Yes, the Earth does turn. So what? The point is simple. Everything starts and ends in the same place. The Earth turns on its axis every 24 plus hours and on that level returns to its former place in that time. The Earth goes around the sun once every 365 or so days and so again finds its own place. Scientists tell us the solar system is part of the Milky Way galaxy and is moving and indeed that the whole of the universe, perhaps, started with some "big bang," which was preceded by nothing.

Let me say all of this in another way. I believe there was a time before time began when everything was in the undifferentiated, unseparated—infinite—All That Is. There will come another time, also beyond time, when All That Is will return to the undifferentiated, unseparated All That Is—otherwise known commonly as God. In essence, we all began from God and will return to God. What's happening in the middle is just your own personal working out of the specifics. This is your path. And this is the core of it. That it must begin and it must end in the All That Is. I may be wrong, but I believe nothing else is possible.

Now, perhaps it is easier to understand why I'm not so concerned with the notion of path. From this perspective, your path will be historically whatever it is you have chosen, consciously or unconsciously, to do in between your separation from the Absolute and your return to the Absolute. To say it another way, you simply cannot stay lost in the desert forever. The very nature of existence will, over time, transform the desert into a garden, and you into a master of that garden.

As I write these words, I hear the objections quite clearly. Isn't this a cop out? Doesn't this allow us to do nothing? What kind of a system is that?

Just try doing nothing. If you sit quietly, you are doing something. If you lie down and go to sleep, you are doing something. If you die, you are doing something. The nature of existence, the fact that you have left the absolute and have consciousness, means you are doing something. There is no way to avoid doing something.

But, you might say, shouldn't I be doing something to move the process along faster? Faster than what? Faster than what you think it should be? Faster than what someone who talks to you thinks it should be? Faster than what?

The movement in the universe has its own rhythms. I can no more redefine those rhythms or change them than I can figure out how many vitamins and minerals to take. But, there is one simple thought I can live my life from that integrates all that has come before in this small volume…

CHAPTER TWELVE

It All Comes Back to Now

Yes, there are general paths that can provide guidance to the seeker for a day, a month, a year or a lifetime, but not forever. The rules of each path are also its limitations and, at some point, each soul will find these limitations to be too burdensome.

The answer is not simply to forget about a path or direction. Having general rules to live by can be very helpful, sometimes essential in any life. The point is to stop giving any path overwhelming importance. It is the road; it only points the way. Your path is your servant, not your master.

The problem is that we become so focused on the journey and getting "**There**" that we lose all the joy of the trip. I have told you that you, indeed all of us, *must* get "**There**." There is no other place to go. You can't get "**There**" any faster by criticizing your progress, worrying whether you are on the right path, or even by analyzing what will move you faster. "**There**" *is not outside you*. It is in your heart, and your path is simply living each moment in a way that lets you feel your heart more and more and more.

If leading a Christian or Buddhist or atheist life does that for you, great. Just remember that, as soon as you start to measure your progress by any external yardstick, whether you have "sinned," whether you are growing as fast as others, or whether you have made a mess of the last few days, years or decades, you are moving away from your heart, you are in your mind or your emotions. The heart runs deeper than either your mind or your emotions.

Your life is in the Present. Your learning is in the Present. Your joy is in the Present. Follow all the rules you wish. Follow any path you wish. But do not criticize yourself. Certainly, self-correct—but do it lightly. Make no moral judgments about yourself. Do not blame or in any way think badly of yourself. Do your best and let it be enough. Anything else will take you out of the Present. Do nothing that takes you out of the Present. When nothing takes you out of each Present moment, you are Home—the eternal Now. The eternal Now is the ongoing expression of Love. Words cannot convey what this means. To appreciate this state, it is necessary to experience it, but let me explain as best I can.

CHAPTER THIRTEEN

LOVE

AT THIS POINT ON THE PATH, the student has long passed the place where actions are responses to pain. No such prods have been necessary for some time. Indeed, by this point, the student is seeking Truth for its own sake, and the rewards for this search on the path are many and manifold. The student has acquired some degree of power. Power is the ability to create change increasingly without trying.

The student has learned to feel and follow what the student increasingly regards as Love, to simplify and purify actions, thoughts and words so that all are very powerful. An abundance of material things is available. It becomes very easy at this point to pay increasing attention to the physical world, to enjoy it for its own sake, to begin to appreciate just how far you have come, and, in short, to take one of a thousand routes that detour away from God and Love.

Love is probably the most overused word in our vocabulary. Young lovers who cannot bear to be parted say "I love you," usually meaning "I need you" and "I want you." A young mother, furious because her child has just spilled grape juice over her best linen, tells herself she must spank the child to teach him a lesson because she loves him. Soldiers go into battle to kill each other because they love their country. Religious leaders urge the persecution of members of other religions because the leaders "love" God. None of this has anything to do with Love. There is no Love expressed in people binding others to them to feel secure or wanted. There is no Love expressed by the person who so loves someone that he cannot live without the other, or by the person who so loves that he will kill "for love." We have made a mockery of love by using that term to mask the bodily passions, worldly desires and the fears of humanity. Love has no place in any of these.

Love is the fabric of creation. It binds the universe together. It is the basic understanding and feeling that you and I are one. The only expression of Love is in giving, never in taking, needing or hurting. For only in giving freely with no thought of return do we give as Divinity gives, and our thoughts, words and actions increasingly partake of Love. This is obviously a very high standard. No one can "will" themselves to meet it. We evolve to it by focusing on love as the source. Learn to find love within. Learn to trust it, and the world will, of its own accord, change around you.

We love to overcomplicate things. But sometimes, a shift happens in an instant—and it's almost annoying how obvious it is in hindsight.

Sarah once told me a story. She'd been sitting next to me after a morning meditation at the retreat house we built. We were just chatting, and I said something offhand: **"The only difference between my worldview and yours is that mine makes me happy and yours doesn't."**

That was it. I wasn't trying to be wise—I was just stating what I believed was a fact.

Years later, she told me that sentence changed her life. Over time, she said she actually did change her worldview—and became happy. Then she looked at me and said, **"If it turns out it was always this easy, I'm going to be really pissed!"**

That's the thing about Love. It's not hiding. It's just not always wearing the costume we expect.

If something stirred in you as you read this book, **trust it, at least long enough to see where it takes you.**

The truth isn't in these words on a page—*it's been in you all along.*

Starting out, I said it was all simple. This has all been said many times before. These are my reflections on my journey in this lifetime.

I wish you the best on your journey. May you find you have nowhere to go and nothing to do.

POSTSCRIPT:

Still a Young New Yorker

Decades after my first stoop in the Bronx, I was walking down a hallway in downtown San Francisco, flanked by two lawyers, when someone spotted me.

"David," they said, "were you just… skipping?"

I was.

We had been speaking Yiddish. And in that moment, I was a kid again. A Bronx boy, loved by Baba, honest as stickball, humming Broadway show tunes with the world.

Turns out, you never really leave home.

Acknowledgements

Acknowledgements usually name individuals whose contributions were so substantial to the creation of the book that, without them, the book would not have been finished. In this case, that is true of each of the following individuals:

My wife Liz urged me to write a book of this nature—so my children and grandchildren could see something of my life in future years. I dawdled for years until I finally remembered the book I had started writing about thirty years ago. I started with that and added—and kept adding.

I had no idea how many people were needed to write a book!

My heartfelt thanks go to:

Janis Baron, who decided to interrupt her retirement to work practically full-time on this project

Dr. Anouk Shambrook, who helped shape the language and familiarized herself with the minutiae of detail required of a publisher to actually get the book done

Kathy Stroud, who jumped in to help with formatting and photos, and to find the expert, Chris Molé, who designed the cover and managed the layout and printing.

I also want to acknowledge Amalya Pomerantz for generously sharing the knowledge she gained from helping her husband David publish his books.

About the Author

DAVID A. ROTMAN grew up in the Bronx, practiced law in San Francisco, and spent decades exploring the nature of reality, love, and human transformation. In 1984, under the guidance of Hilda Charlton, he began teaching meditation—a path that led to a lifelong practice of presence, inquiry, and community.

He is depicted in the photo above on the left, seated with his best friend and teacher, David Pomerantz.

His work draws on a deep well of lived experience, from spiritual study to parenting, from courtroom litigation to quiet mornings of stillness.

David lives with his wife, Liz, and two children, continuing to walk the path with introspection, love and humor.

To connect or learn more, email:
davidarotmanbooks@gmail.com

www.ingramcontent.com/pod-product-compliance
Lightning Source LLC
Chambersburg PA
CBHW040237110526
44582CB00022B/218/J